A Pocket Guide to
Biking
on Mount Desert Island
2nd Edition

BY **AUDREY MINUTOLO LE**
MAPS BY **RUTH ANN HILL**

Down East Books

ISBN 978-1-60893-046-3

Cover photograph by Eco Photography

Printed in the United States

Down East Books
www.nbnbooks.com
Distributed by National Book Network

CONTENTS

Foreword

About halfway up the rocky coast of Maine lies the island of Mount Desert, home of Acadia National Park. Like anyone who loves the outdoors, I find the island's landscape breathtakingly beautiful, but for me Mount Desert Island holds much more than just the beauty of the national park or the stunning landscape and ocean views. Indeed, this island holds a special place in my heart, for Mount Desert Island is not only home to Acadia National Park, it has been home to my family for four generations.

Because of its welcoming natural beauty and its accessibility for all outdoor activities, Acadia is special for everyone who travels here. In fact, visitors have access to what sets Acadia apart from other national parks: its unique 57-mile interconnected network of carriage roads. These roads were the brainchild of John D. Rockefeller, Jr. who, in his quest to escape the early twentieth century industrial automobile, created the carriage roads for non-motorized use only. Those early horseless wagons—with their noise and racy names like 'roadster' and 'runabout'—certainly did not hold much appeal to Rockefeller, who wanted to preserve and protect the natural landscape surrounding his summer home on the island. We are fortunate to have this legacy of carriage roads, as well as the idyllic stone bridges and English Tudor stone gatehouses that accompany them; such stone architecture only enhances and reflects what is natural in this bucolic setting. In conjunction with Rockefeller's foresight to create the carriage roads, the ambitious efforts of George B. Dorr and Charles Eliot helped preserve and protect the pristine beauty of the island by establishing a national park here in 1919. Equally notable efforts of many other nature lovers and landscape architects, including Beatrix Farrand, Frederick Law Olmstead, and Charles Savage, have left a lasting imprint of natural elegance and the simplicity of a bygone era.

Today, bicyclists have become as much a part of the landscape as the lakes and mountains, and the bicycling terrain available on Mount Desert Island is as diverse as its surroundings. Because the carriage roads are open only to bicyclists, equestrians, and pedestrians, they are the penultimate setting to take family bike rides; just as was true more than one hundred years ago, the carriage roads are safe from the dangers of cars.

Other stunningly scenic roads and picturesque villages on Mount Desert Island extend beyond the boundaries of the national park and provide perfect riding for the cycling enthusiast. Backcountry roads and gravel state 'fire' roads wind past mountains, fields, and farms, and along the shores of lakes and the ocean, offering a never-ending network for bicycling.

Whether bicycling for transportation or recreation, in sun or in fog, it is my hope that others will enjoy and appreciate riding in this beautiful setting.

Introduction

This book is designed to help bicyclists of all ages and skill levels choose rides most appropriate for their abilities. Each description offers information about mileage and gives a generalized skill rating. Detailed maps show all the routes.

These rides do not stay just within the perimeters of Acadia National Park, but encompass the entire island. Although the park and carriage roads are especially beautiful and comprise the most popularly visited portion of Mount Desert Island, other areas of the island are equally scenic. Some of the rides follow state or town roads along the coast or through rural countryside. Cycling various parts of Mount Desert Island will give you a greater scope for viewing this rocky coastal island.

Bicycling in Acadia

FAMILY RIDING

The rating system within this book often refers to "Family" rides. Although the rating is based on children of eight years of age and older, or infants riding in bicycle seats, it is best to use your own judgment about your children's abilities. Trailers, carts, or tag-a-long trailers are a great way to ride with young children, but be aware that some segments of these rides may include roads that have automobile traffic. Always plan for your youngest or weakest cyclist. The safest and most appropriate riding for families is on the carriage roads within Acadia National Park.

Other areas to bicycle in Acadia National Park are the fire roads: Long Pond Fire Road, Seal Cove Road, Western Mountain Road, Lurvey Spring Road, and Man O' War Brook Road. Although traffic is allowed on these gravel roads (except Man O' War Brook Road), which are located on the western side of the island, the maximum speed is only 15 mph, making these safe areas to ride as well.

Wherever you decide to explore, plan accordingly and establish rules within your riding group before embarking: (1)

Read the Rules of the Road to your group so that everyone knows the benchmarks for safe and responsible riding, and (2) Wait for the rest of your group at each signpost or intersection to ensure that your riding party stays together.

OFF-ROAD RIDING/MOUNTAIN BIKING

Bicyclists who love the challenge of off-road riding (or single-track riding, as it is also known) spend much of their time exploring pathways and trails that cut through the wilderness. As appealing as the hiking trails throughout the park may look, riding on these trails is not allowed. Delicate tree-root systems become damaged and trails erode, so please heed the rules.

Although there is no single-track or off-road riding available on Mount Desert Island, the carriage roads and fire roads offer excellent mountain biking.

TOURING AND ROAD RIDING

The rural roads that wind throughout Mount Desert Island's farmland, meadows, and villages—as well as the ever-popular Park Loop Road—provide challenging and scenic riding for the serious cyclist. Many of these rural roads do not have bike lanes, however. Exercise caution, and wear bright riding clothing and reflectives for safety. Road or touring bikes are not appropriate for the gravel-surfaced carriage roads or fire roads; the wider tires on mountain or cross-terrain bikes are better suited for these roads.

BICYCLING ISSUES IN ACADIA

In recent years, increasing numbers of bicyclists, walkers, and horseback riders have all been exploring Acadia's carriage roads. Conflicts can occur if individuals from these user groups are uninformed about the rules of the carriage roads. In 1994, such a case of misunderstanding and lack of consideration resulted in a ban on 13 miles of carriage roads that lie on private property. Irresponsible actions by a few have threatened the privileges of many. Therefore, bicyclists should always yield to pedestrians and equestrians; a speeding bicycle can truly shock others who are enjoying the peaceful tranquility the natural world.

The Downeast Bicycle Club is one of several organizations working to educate and promote responsible and fun cycling. They welcome all ages, abilities, and interests. Call 207-288-3886 for more information.

COURTESIES AND RULES OF THE ROAD

It is important to remember that all visitors, whether riding, walking, or horseback riding, want an enjoyable experience. As outdoor recreationists, whatever your interest, please be gracious visitors while on park property. Do your part by adhering to the Rules of the Road (below) and by riding responsibly. Also, access the park by bicycle or by using the Island Explorer bus service whenever possible to help ease the burden of congested roads and parking areas in Acadia. Adhering to basic courtesies and practicing safe, responsible riding is the key to the future of bicycling privileges everywhere.

RULES OF THE ROAD
Courtesy of the International Mountain Biking Association (IMBA):

1. **Stay on the carriage roads or paved roads.** Hiking trails are off limits to bicyclists.
2. **Stay to the right.** Keep carriage roads clear for others to pass.
3. **Always yield to others.** When approaching others, give a friendly greeting and pass slowly on the left. When approaching horses, do not use bells and do use extra caution when passing.

4. Ride in control. Carriage roads have loose gravel surfaces that make fast stops difficult. Control your speed, and be prepared to stop.

5. Leave no trace. Carry out what you carry in, and don't litter while you're there.

You will also see signs posted at the carriage road gates that reiterate the IMBA rules and inform users of other carriage road rules:

- Ride and walk on the right.
- Warn others when passing from behind.
- Control your speed! Stay alert.
- Use caution around horses.
- Keep dogs on a leash.
- No bicycles or horses on hiking trails or off-road.
- Stay away from all wildlife and do not ever feed the animals.

For your own safety and that of others:

1. Wear a helmet.

2. Wear high-visibility clothing.

3. Use maps. The maps in this book facilitate easy navigation. It may only be an island, but if you get lost it could be a very long ride home.

4. Carry water.

5. Dress for the weather. Coastal Maine weather is changeable, and temperatures on the mountains or near the water are always cooler. Layering is always the best method.

NOTES ABOUT POPULAR ROUTES

All of Mount Desert Island is breathtakingly scenic, but proximity to Bar Harbor has made Witch Hole Pond and Eagle Lake so popular during the summer months that alternative rides may be more enjoyable. Explore some of the other routes described in this book for less crowded conditions.

Because of its marshy topography, Aunt Betty Pond tends to have a heavy horsefly population in July. Topical deterrents—bug spray—may help, but alternate routes near the lakes or ocean may be a better way to avoid the bugs.

Most important, please *avoid taking small children on rides that involve paved-road riding*. Because many state, town, and park roads do not have paved shoulders, heavy summer traffic creates dangerous riding conditions for little ones. Carriage road routes are a safer alternative.

OTHER AREAS OF ACADIA NATIONAL PARK: SCHOODIC and ISLE au HAUT

It is important to note that Acadia National Park also includes areas at Schoodic Point and the rural coastal island of Isle au Haut. The Schoodic area can be reached by car, but Isle au Haut is accessible only by mail boat from the fishing port of Stonington on Deer Isle. Although these smaller areas of Acadia National Park are not on Mount Desert Island, they hold possibilities for adventures you won't soon forget.

WEATHER AND ROAD CONDITIONS

Coastal Maine weather can be unpredictable; even the meteorologists sometimes make inaccurate predictions. Although the island's location along the coast offers relatively moderate temperatures, the wind often blows from the northwest, bringing in cold air from Canada. Fog and rain are common, so be prepared with extra clothing.

Road conditions vary throughout the island. The best road surfaces are those of the Park Loop Road, Route 102, Crooked Road, and most of Route 233/Eagle Lake Road. Although portions of Eagle Lake Road have bike lanes, traffic is busy and fast on this road; it may be better to find an alternate route. Bicycle awareness is increasing among drivers, but wearing bright reflective clothing will alert drivers to your presence.

Information and Resources

INFORMATION

Local bicycle shops regularly show short informational videos to promote safe, responsible riding and give visiting riders educational tips. Contact any of the following resources for information about bicycling on Mount Desert Island or for information about the island itself.

Abbe Museum Native American Stone Age Antiquities
Bar Harbor   288-3519
www.abbemuseum.org

Acadia National Park Headquarters
Eagle Lake Road, Bar Harbor   288-3639
www.nps.gov/acad

Bar Harbor Chamber of Commerce
Bar Harbor   288-5103
www.barharborinfo.com

Bar Harbor Historical Society
Bar Harbor   288-0000
www.barharborhistorical.org

Island Explorer Bus Service & Downeast Transportation
Ellsworth   667-5796
www.exploreacadia.com

Jesup Library
Bar Harbor   288-4245
www.jesup.lib.me.us

Down East Bicycle Club
Bar Harbor   288-3886
http://downeastbicycleclub.ning.com/

Friends of Acadia
Bar Harbor   288-3340
www.friendsofacadia.org

Mount Desert Chamber of Commerce
Mount Desert   276-5040
www.mountdesertchamber.org

Southwest Harbor/Tremont Chamber of Commerce
Southwest Harbor   244-9264
www.acadiachamber.com

GOODS AND SERVICES

For purchases or rental of equipment, repairs, or information, there are several bicycle shops on the island. If, by unfortunate chance, you have mechanical difficulty on the trails, go to the nearest town for assistance.

Acadia Bike and Canoe Company
Bar Harbor   288-9605
www.acadiabike.com

Bar Harbor Bicycle Shop
Bar Harbor   288-3886
www.barharborbike.com

Island Bike Rental
Northeast Harbor   276-5611

Southwest Cycle
Southwest Harbor   244-5856
www.southwestcycle.com

CAMPING

What better way to explore the Maine coast than by bicycling by day and camping at night? There are a number of campgrounds on Mount Desert Island, some of which are located within Acadia National Park, as indicated below. Please be aware that some campgrounds also accommodate large RVs, so if you're looking for a more 'primitive' camping experience, be sure to ask. Campgrounds within Acadia National Park are indicated by *. For all National Parks & Forest Service campground reservations, go to www.recreation.gov or call Acadia National Park Headquarters: 207-288-3338, or call the campground directly, as listed below.

Bar Harbor Campground
Bar Harbor   288-5185
www.thebarharborcampground.com

Bar Harbor/KOA Oceanside Campground
Bar Harbor   288-3520
http://koa.com/campgrounds/bar-harbor-oceanside

Blackwoods Campground/Acadia National Park
Otter Creek   288-3274
www.nps.gov/acad/planyourvisit/campgrounds.htm

Duck Harbor Campground/Acadia National Park
Isle au Haut   288-3338
www.nps.gov/acad/planyourvisit/campgrounds.htm

Hadley's Point Campground
Bar Harbor   288-4808
www.hadleyspoint.com

Mount Desert Campground
Mount Desert   244-3710
www.mountdesertcampground.com

Mount Desert Narrows Camping Resort
Bar Harbor   288-4782
www.barharborcampingresorts.com

Smuggler's Den Campground & Cabins
Southwest Harbor   877-244-9033
www.smugglersdencampground.com

Seawall Campground/Acadia National Park
Southwest Harbor   244-3600
www.nps.gov/acad/planyourvisit/campgrounds.htm

Somes Sound View Campground
Mount Desert   244-3890
www.ssvc.info

Mount Desert Island

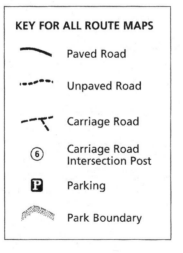

KEY FOR ALL ROUTE MAPS

- Paved Road
- Unpaved Road
- Carriage Road
- ⑥ Carriage Road Intersection Post
- 🅿 Parking
- Park Boundary

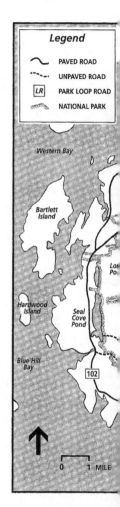

Legend

- PAVED ROAD
- UNPAVED ROAD
- *LR* PARK LOOP ROAD
- NATIONAL PARK

Western Bay

Bartlett Island

Hardwood Island

Seal Cove Pond

Blue Hill Bay

Lor Po.

102

0   1 MILE

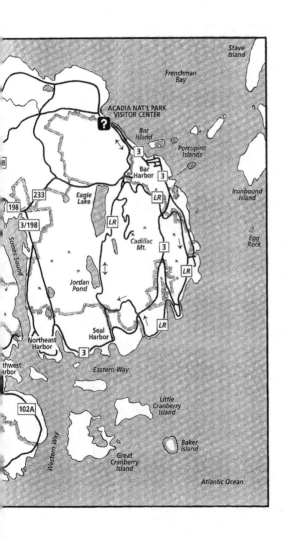

MAP 1: WITCH HOLE POND LOOP

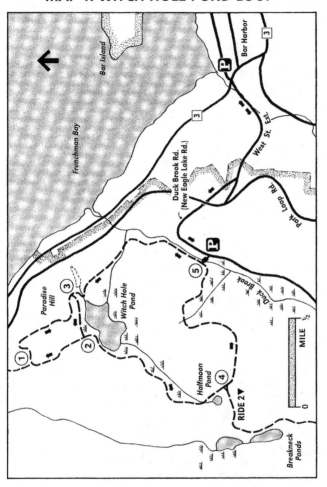

Carriage Road Rides

1

Witch Hole Pond Loop, Paradise Hill Loop

3.4 miles, or 4.6 miles including Paradise Hill (*Easy/Family*)

The Witch Hole Pond carriage road offers a comfortably short loop with moderate terrain, which is ideal for family riding. The loop is within proximity of the village of Bar Harbor and is interconnected with the Eagle Lake Loop and Paradise Hill Loop for longer rides. Be aware, however, that the appeal of this loop can create congestion in the peak summer months.

For a more moderate excursion, begin this ride by parking at the carriage road gates at Duck Brook. Or you can access this route directly from Bar Harbor by riding the incline west on West Street Extension through the park gates. Take a right at Duck Brook Road (New Eagle Lake Road) and follow the road to the parking area at the carriage road entrance.

The granite triple-arched bridge at Duck Brook brings you

into the carriage road system. Take a right at Post 5 at the end of the bridge, and coast down the hill. A word of caution to families with young children: There are sections with steep drop-offs on the right-hand side, so keep children to your left.

Follow the curve in the road to the left, which takes you through a small marsh. The top of the next hill reveals another small lily pad-dotted wetland on the right, and Witch Hole Pond on the left. Signs of wildlife—including ducks, beavers, and an occasional great blue heron—can usually be seen near the marshes and pond.

At the end of the short, steep climb past the wetlands is Post 3. Turn left, and ride to the next intersection, marked Post 2. If you wish to continue your ride around Witch Hole Pond Loop only, bear left at Post 2.

If you'd like to take the Paradise Hill Loop, turn right at Post 2. This route capitalizes on the expansive views of Hulls Cove and Frenchman Bay. Pass by Post 1, which leads to the Acadia National Park Visitor Center in Hulls Cove, and climb the hill to the vista overlooking Hulls Cove. Continue around Paradise Hill, finishing at Post 3. Ride back to Post 2, backtracking over a short distance, then continue on around Witch Hole Pond.

At Post 4, you can, if you wish, continue on to Eagle Lake. (See Eagle Lake Loop, p.28)

To stay on the Witch Hole Pond Loop, proceed along the gradual incline. At the end of the straight stretch of road is an open view of Sargent and Cadillac Mountains and a rewarding downhill. The remainder of the ride is on level terrain, finishing at the Duck Brook Bridge.

This route interconnects with: the Paradise Hill Loop (best route at Post 2) or Ride #2, Eagle Lake Loop (at Post 4). Note that there is no swimming allowed at Eagle Lake, Bubble Pond, or Jordan Pond.

2

Eagle Lake Loop

6 miles (*Moderate/Family*)

As with the Witch Hole Pond Loop, striking scenery and proximity to Bar Harbor have made the 6-mile Eagle Lake Loop a popular ride—so much so that during peak summer months, the crowds can detract from the wilderness experience. But, indeed, the convenience to connect with other routes, the lake breezes, and the views as you journey around the lake are well worth the ride any time of year.

Beginning from the Eagle Lake parking lot on Route 233/ Eagle Lake Road, go to the intersection and turn left under the granite bridge, and ride straight ahead along the west side of Eagle Lake, passing Post 6 and then Post 9, which leads to Aunt Betty Pond.

Approximately 2 miles from the starting point, the carriage road begins a long ascent that branches away from the lake's shore and into the woods. At the top of the hill stands Post 8.

MAP 2: EAGLE LAKE LOOP

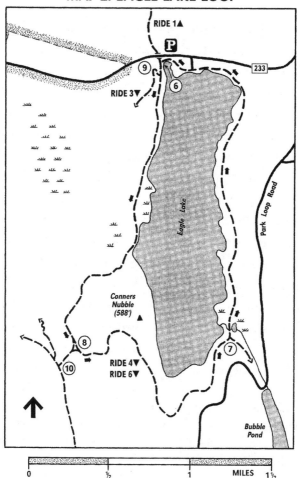

To get to Jordan Pond, go straight from Post 8 for 0.2 mile and turn left at Post 10. The Jordan Pond House is a 2.5-mile ride from Post 10. For an alternate route, take a right at Post 10 onto the Around-the-Mountain Loop, which also leads to Jordan Pond House and adds 11 spectacular, but hilly, miles to your ride.

To continue around Eagle Lake, go left at Post 8 and follow the curving road through the woods. This section has various inclines and descents, including a particularly long downhill that lasts nearly a mile.

Bear left at Post 7, where you'll again catch glimpses of Eagle Lake. This segment of carriage road is wooded and peaceful. You will cross a small bridge that spans a mountain stream. Continue straight along the east side of the lake. The carriage road bears a sharp left at the north end of the lake, passing through the park gates at the boat landing and back to the starting point at Post 6.

This route interconnects with: Ride #3, the Aunt Betty Pond Loop (at Post 9); Ride #4, Bubble Pond/Triad/Jordan Pond Loop (at Post 8); and Ride #7, the Around-the-Mountain Loop (at Post 8). Note that there is no swimming allowed at Eagle Lake, Bubble Pond, or Jordan Pond.

3

Aunt Betty Pond Loop, Giant Slide Loop

6 miles (*Moderate*)

Either direction around the Aunt Betty Pond Loop has steep climbs, but your efforts will be rewarded by its lovely pastoral setting and beautiful scenery. This carriage road winds through the woods, past meadows and marshes, with a rigorous climb up a series of bridges over Chasm Brook.

The easiest-to-access and safest route begins from the Eagle Lake parking lot off Route 233. Turn left under the Eagle Lake Road bridge, and stay to the right of Post 6. At the next intersection, Post 9, turn right onto the Aunt Betty Pond Loop. This is the first of this ride's two lengthy climbs. At the top of the hill is a lovely view of Eagle Lake, Cadillac Mountain, Aunt Betty Pond, and Blue Hill Mountain in the distance.

After a long, gradual descent, the road passes by Aunt Betty Pond, which lies to the right. The pond's water level varies with the seasons; the banks flood in spring, whereas in the summer heat the water level drops considerably.

MAP 3: AUNT BETTY POND LOOP
GIANT SLIDE LOOP

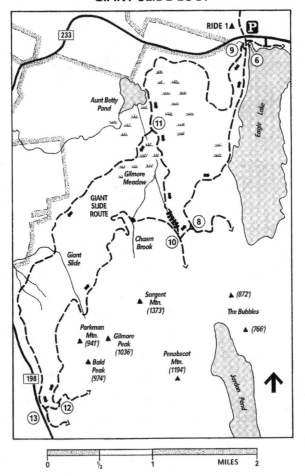

RIDE 1

233

Aunt Betty Pond

Eagle Lake

Gilmore Meadow

GIANT SLIDE ROUTE

Giant Slide

Chasm Brook

Sargent Mtn. (1373')

▲ (872')

The Bubbles

▲ (766')

Parkman Mtn. ▲ (941')

Gilmore Peak (1036')

Bald Peak ▲ (974')

Penobscot Mtn. (1194')

Jordan Pond

198

0   ½   1   MILES   2

After leaving the shores of the pond, you'll see the intersection with the Giant Slide Loop at Post 11. Bearing right at this point stretches the ride from 6 miles to 12.8 miles. If you choose to do so, follow the directions for Giant Slide Loop, below.

To continue around Aunt Betty Pond, turn left at Post 11. Gilmore Meadow, on the right, provides habitat for a variety of birds and animals, and marks the beginning of the Seven Bridges segment.

You will be pedaling over Chasm Brook and crossing not seven, but six bridges. Downshift and prepare for a climb. Enjoy the scenery of this quaint countryside, but be prepared for other riders or hikers approaching in the opposite direction.

Turn left at the next junction, Post 10, and begin a welcome long descent back toward the shoreline of Eagle Lake. Bear left at the triangle, Post 8. Be sure to check your speed through here; riders and pedestrians may be coming from the other direction. Follow the carriage road on the western side of Eagle Lake, and conclude the ride back at Post 6.

The Aunt Betty Pond ride interconnects with the Giant Slide Loop as follows: At Post 11, turn right. Follow the carriage road for about 3 miles. Turn left at Post 13, and left again at Posts 12 and 10, respectively. Stay to the left of Post 8, and return on the west side of Eagle Lake.
Note that there is no swimming allowed at Eagle Lake, Bubble Pond, or Jordan Pond.

4

Bubble Pond/Jordan Pond Loop

8.6 miles (13.5 miles from Bar Harbor) (*Moderate to Difficult*)

This loop was the focus of the carriage road restoration project in 1995; its smooth gravel surface reflects the commitment of Acadia National Park and the Friends of Acadia to continuing this important preservation of the carriage road system.

One of the best ways to enjoy this ride is to take most of the day to savor the sights, leaving from Bar Harbor in the morning and returning in the afternoon. The first part of this route combines part of the Witch Hole Pond Loop and follows the west side of Eagle Lake, turning left at Post 8 and interconnecting with the Bubble Pond/Jordan Pond Loop by turning right at Post 7. The total mileage, starting from Bar Harbor, is about 13.5 miles.

You can, however, ride just this loop by starting at the Bubble Pond parking lot. The loop begins along the western shore of Bubble Pond and winds for 2.5 miles along the base of Pemetic Mountain. This portion of the carriage road cuts

MAP 4: BUBBLE POND/JORDAN POND LOOP

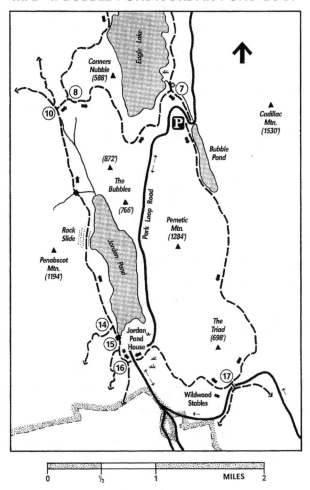

Eagle Lake

Conners Nubble
(588')

8

10

(872')

The Bubbles

(766')

Rock Slide

Penobscot Mtn.
(1194')

Jordan Pond

14

15

Jordan Pond House

16

7

P

Bubble Pond

Cadillac Mtn.
(1530')

Park Loop Road

Pemetic Mtn.
(1284')

The Triad
(698')

17

Wildwood Stables

0   ½   1   MILES   2

through mostly wooded forest where there are some longer climbs and gradual descents.

Stay to the right at Post 17, and Wildwood Stables will appear below on your left. The Park Loop Road intersects the carriage road system 1 mile from Post 17. Pass through the gateposts, and cross the road where the carriage road system picks up again on the other side. Bear right at Post 16. Coast gently and slowly down this hill; it flanks the Jordan Pond House, and a substantial number of visitors turn onto the carriage road from other trails.

You will pass by Post 15, and then the carriage road curves sharply left, crossing over Jordan Stream. Keep right at Post 14. A slight downhill grade gives you a chance to prepare for the next mile, which is a steady climb as the carriage road cuts through the side of Penobscot Mountain. The view of Jordan Pond to your right, below, and the enormous boulders of the Jordan Cliffs rock slide to your left, will help keep your mind off your work as you climb the hill.

Turn right at Post 10, and again at Post 8, for a long descent that will bring you to Post 7. Turn right again, following the incline to the Park Loop Road, and conclude your ride across the road at the Bubble Pond parking lot.

Note that there is no swimming allowed at Eagle Lake, Bubble Pond, or Jordan Pond.

5

Upper Hadlock and Cedar Swamp Mountain Loop

3.8 miles (*Easy/Family*)

This short loop near Northeast Harbor offers a sampling of the highlights of all the carriage roads. Three granite bridges and mountain, lake, and ocean views can be seen at points along the carriage road, making this a most rewarding ride.

From Route 198 traveling south toward Northeast Harbor, park at the Parkman Mountain parking lot, tucked in on the left at the rise before Upper Hadlock Pond.

At the carriage road entrance, turn right, then bear left at Post 13 and ride the gradual incline on the winding carriage road. This climb requires effort, but around each corner the scenery opens up to reveal increasingly breathtaking views. Take a right at Post 12, where the road levels off at a higher elevation. Be cautious of others on the hairpin curve here.

Where Parkman Mountain Trail crosses the road, views of Upper Hadlock Pond and Norumbega Mountain dominate the foreground, with a glimpse of outer islands and Western Way in the distance.

MAP 5: UPPER HADLOCK/CEDAR SWAMP MOUNTAIN LOOP

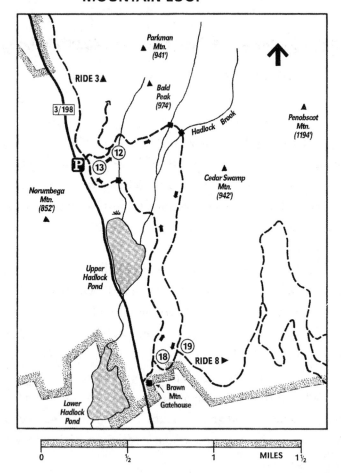

Parkman
Mtn.
(941')

Bald
Peak
(974')

RIDE 3▲

3/198

Hadlock Brook

Penobscot
Mtn.
(1194')

12

P

13

Cedar Swamp
Mtn.
(942')

Norumbega
Mtn.
(852')

Upper
Hadlock
Pond

19

18

RIDE 8 ▶

Brown
Mtn.
Gatehouse

Lower
Hadlock
Pond

0   ½   1   MILES   1½

The picturesque Deer Brook Bridge comes into view, immediately followed by the Waterfall Bridge; Maple Spring Trail and Hadlock Brook Trail, respectively, cross the road at these bridge points. In 1925, John D. Rockefeller, Jr. oversaw the work of local stonemasons as they made these bridges from granite blocks extracted nearby.

These bridges mark the beginning of a wonderfully long downhill ride on the side of Cedar Swamp Mountain (also referred to as the Sargent Mountain carriage road), with frequent views of Norumbega to the right

Bear right at Post 19, and right again at Post 18. A short detour to the left at Post 19 will take you to Brown Mountain Gatehouse, designed by architect Grosvenor Atterbury in French Provincial style and well worth seeing.

Beginning again from Post 18, the narrower carriage road follows along the eastern shore of Upper Hadlock Pond for a short distance. The smaller scale of the Hadlock Brook Bridge seems appropriate for a fairy-tale setting, and is a perfect spot to stop and absorb the sights and sounds of the surrounding woods.

The carriage road follows a gradual incline back to Post 13. Bear left, and take a left at the gate back to the parking lot.

This route interconnects with: part of Ride #3, the Giant Slide Loop (at Post 13); or Ride #8, the Amphitheater Loop (at Post 19).

6

Day Mountain Loop

6.3 miles (*Moderate/Family*)

The Day Mountain Loop passes through sloping terrain along a shaded wilderness carriage road. This can be an optimal family ride, and the view at the top is spectacular. Remember, though, that bicyclists must always yield to horses, and that the summer horse traffic can make for some very bumpy riding through loose gravel. This loop can be ridden in conjunction with Ride #4 (Bubble Pond/Jordan Pond Loop, pps 34–36).

This route begins at the Jordan Pond House. You can park at the Jordan Pond House or ride your bike there via the Park Loop Road. Turn right out of the Pond House parking area onto the Park Loop Road for 0.1 mile to Jordan Pond Gatehouse. Turn left, entering the carriage road system. The first mile of carriage road follows along the southern edge of Pemetic Mountain, where dramatic granite cliffs border the road on your left. Wildwood Stables will appear on your right. Follow the carriage

MAP 6: DAY MOUNTAIN LOOP

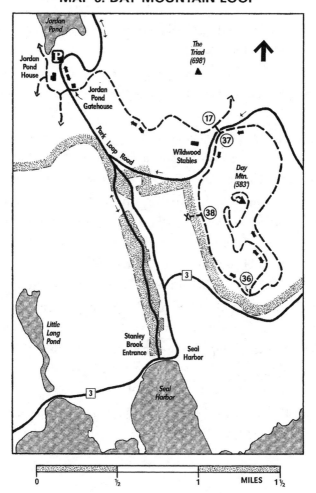

Jordan Pond

The Triad (698')

Jordan Pond House

Jordan Pond Gatehouse

Park Loop Road

17

37

Wildwood Stables

Day Mtn. (583')

38

3

36

Little Long Pond

Stanley Brook Entrance

Seal Harbor

Seal Harbor

3

0   ½   1   MILES   1½

road to Post 17, and turn right to cross the granite bridge that spans the Park Loop Road.

Post 37 marks the beginning of the Day Mountain Loop. Turn right and follow the winding carriage road around the mountain. There are few scenic vistas throughout the old forest that blankets the mountain, but in early spring and late fall the bare deciduous trees allow frequent glimpses of the surrounding mountains. The first mile slopes downhill and levels off as you continue straight past Post 38. Once past the intersection, however, a quick downshift will help your ascent up the next hill.

Post 36 marks the intersection with the Day Mountain summit road. This curving road offers increasing views as it climbs to the top, ending at the 583-foot summit. Descend the same route, and turn left at Post 36 to continue the ride. The summit road comes into view several times as you ride along below. You can complete the remainder of the tree-lined loop back at Post 37.

Turn right at Post 37 and cross the granite bridge. Turn left at Post 17 and follow the same route back, concluding your ride at Jordan Pond Gatehouse.

7

Around-the-Mountain Loop

15 miles (including access from Eagle Lake)
(*Moderate to Difficult*)

"Mountain" in the title is somewhat misleading; by the time you complete this loop, you will have circumnavigated not one, but several mountains, including Sargent, Parkman, Cedar Swamp, and Penobscot. The climbs can be a tough workout, but the expansive vistas at the top of each are well worth the effort.

Begin at the Eagle Lake parking lot. Bear right at Post 6 and ride the west side of Eagle Lake along the shore and up the hill into the woods. At Post 8, bear right and turn right again at Post 10, heading up the side of Sargent Mountain. The notable landmarks along the way are Chasm Brook Bridge and switchbacks in the road approaching the top. The nearly 2-mile climb gives way to a spectacular panoramic view of Somes Sound with the Camden Hills in the distance.

As you descend, the woods on Sargent Mountain are the

MAP 7: AROUND-THE-MOUNTAIN LOOP

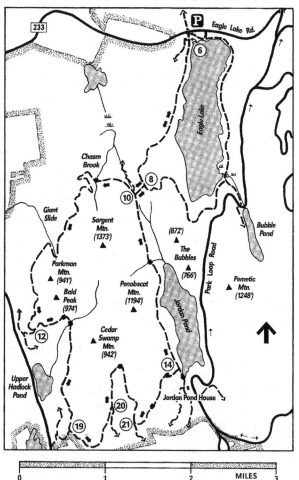

233

P Eagle Lake Rd.

6

Eagle Lake

Chasm Brook

8

10

Giant Slide

Sargent Mtn. (1373')

(872')

The Bubbles

(766')

Bubble Pond

Parkman Mtn. (941')

Bald Peak (974')

Penobscot Mtn. (1194')

Jordan Pond

Park Loop Road

Pemetic Mtn. (1248')

12

Cedar Swamp Mtn. (942')

14

Upper Hadlock Pond

19

20

21

Jordan Pond House

0   1   2   MILES   3

delight of any botanical observer: pitch pines, cedars, maples, birches, laurels, and wild blueberries come together to form a stunning natural garden landscape.

Continue straight past Post 12, and bear left at Post 19, beginning the ascent of Cedar Swamp Mountain. Bear left again at Post 20; this will take you along the upper Amphitheater Loop, where you will cross the Amphitheater Bridge.

Turn left at Post 21. This route skirts the eastern rim of Penobscot Mountain, over two more granite bridges, and down to Post 14. Here you can take a right for the Jordan Pond House, where luncheon or tea and popovers are served every day from May through October. The building also has facilities and water fountains.

If you choose to just continue your ride, turn left at Post 14; this takes you along the edge of Jordan Cliffs overlooking Jordan Pond. Beyond the rock slide and breathtaking views of Jordan Pond, the road levels off under a canopy of beech trees.

At Post 10, turn right and then bear left at Post 8, following your original route along the western shore of Eagle Lake back to the parking lot. Again, please note that there is no swimming allowed at Eagle Lake, Bubble Pond, or Jordan Pond.

8

Amphitheater Loop

5 miles (*Easy/Family*)

The Amphitheater Loop offers nature's quiet solitude for a leisurely cycling experience. Acoustics of the natural amphitheater
gently carry bird calls and other sounds through the forest as
you wind your way along the carriage road.

From Northeast Harbor, go north on Route 198 to the
Brown Mountain Gatehouse parking lot. To access the carriage
road, follow a gentle hill to Post 18, and turn right. The road
continues gently uphill, then levels off until you come to Post 19,
at which point you turn right again. As you follow the incline,
you'll begin to see glimpses of Western Way and the Cranberry
Isles off to the right.

After bearing left at Post 20, the road leads to the expansive
Amphitheater Bridge where it crosses Little Harbor Brook. From
here the road travels through evergreen forest to the south and
winds down the hill. At Post 21, stay to the right; a left would

MAP 8: AMPHITHEATER LOOP

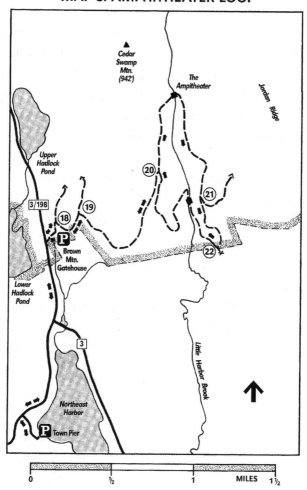

Cedar Swamp Mtn. (942')

The Ampitheater

Jordan Ridge

Upper Hadlock Pond

3/198

20

21

19

18

P

Brown Mtn. Gatehouse

22

Lower Hadlock Pond

3

Little Harbor Brook

Northeast Harbor

P Town Pier

0   ½   1   MILES   1½

take you past Penobscot Mountain and eventually to the Jordan Pond House. Along this segment of the carriage road, there are large rocks on the surface. Keep your pace slow; the grade of the hill may make you want to go fast, but loose gravel and tight turns make quick stops almost impossible at higher speeds.

Travel around to the right again at Post 22. The carriage road follows a straight stretch along the picturesque Little Harbor Brook to the Little Harbor Brook Bridge.

Once you have crossed the bridge, you will need to begin downshifting. The carriage road rises through the woods for more than 0.5 mile, with only a short respite of level riding. The views and wilderness experience throughout these woods are worth the climb.

At Post 20, turn left and follow the carriage road back toward Post 19, reversing your original direction.

Paved and Carriage Road Combination Rides

9

Eagle Lake and the Mountain Road Loop

9 miles (*Moderate*)

Beginning from the town of Bar Harbor, this ride combines paved roads and carriage roads with lake breezes and mountain views. Ride 0.7 mile up West Street Extension, through the park gates, and take a right at Duck Brook Road (New Eagle Lake Road). Follow the road under the arched granite bridge of the Park Loop Road overpass and around the left-hand curve. You will pass the entrance to the carriage road system, but continue on the paved road for the length of Duck Brook Road, 1.9 miles.

At the intersection of Route 233/Eagle Lake Road, take a right and ride 0.2 mile, then take a left at the carriage road entrance and boat landing at Eagle Lake. Turn left onto the carriage road, following the eastern shore of Eagle Lake. At Post 7, turn left and ride to where the carriage road intersects with the paved Park Loop

MAP 9: EAGLE LAKE/MOUNTAIN ROAD LOOP

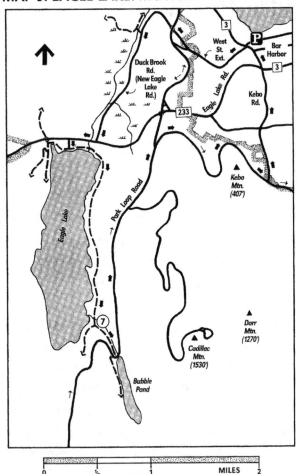

Duck Brook Rd. (New Eagle Lake Rd.)

West St. Ext.

Bar Harbor

3

3

Eagle Lake Rd.

Kebo Rd.

233

Kebo Mtn. (407')

Eagle Lake

Park Loop Road

Dorr Mtn. (1270')

Cadillac Mtn. (1530')

7

Bubble Pond

0   ½   1   MILES   2

Road. Across the road is Bubble Pond, a tranquil spot for picnicking or relaxing, and worth the short detour. Note that there is no swimming allowed at Eagle Lake, Bubble Pond, or Jordan Pond.

From Eagle Lake, turn left (east) onto the Park Loop Road. This begins an uphill climb along the lower elevations of Cadillac Mountain. The grade of this two-way road segment is gradual, although traffic can be heavy during the summer months. An expansive view of Eagle Lake and the surrounding landscape are ample reward for completing the climb.

You will pass the entrance of the summit road up Cadillac Mountain and then come to a fork in the road. Stay to the right, following the signs for the Park Loop Road and Sand Beach. At the overlook parking area, take in the magnificent view of Frenchman Bay and the Porcupine Islands before you begin the long descent on the Park Loop Road. You will pass the Gorge Path (which goes between Cadillac and Dorr Mountains) and the Dorr Mountain North Ridge Trail.

The Park Loop Road makes a turn to the left, after which is an unmarked paved road (Kebo Road) on the left. Turn left and follow Kebo Road through the golf course. Cross over Cromwell Harbor Road, and continue up the hill on Kebo Road. Follow the steep descent to the stop sign at the intersection of Route 233 and Route 3. Cross the intersection onto Route 3 (West), which will bring you back to West Street Extension, where you began the ride.

10

Sargent Drive

10.7 miles (*Difficult*)

This route combines both on- and off-road riding and a glimpse of a geological phenomenon left by the Laurentide Ice Sheet that covered the island 20,000 years ago: Somes Sound, the only fjord on the East Coast.

You can begin this ride in Northeast Harbor by parking at the municipal parking lot at the town pier and marina at the end of Harbor Lane. From the town pier, ride past the Kimball Terrace Inn and Huntington Place Condominiums. Turn right onto South Shore Road, where you will ride through a neighborhood of graceful, old summer cottages. After 0.7 mile, the road becomes Manchester Road and continues for 1.1 miles, winding through more of the historic district.

At the intersection of Manchester Road and Mill Brook Road, turn left and follow the road past the golf course onto Sargent Drive. This segment of road begs the attention of anyone

MAP 10: SARGENT DRIVE

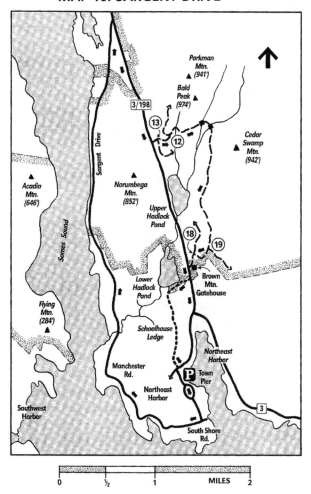

with an appetite for country roads that wind along the edge of the sea. Its beauty is striking, but be sure to keep your safety wits about you, as there is no shoulder and sometimes limited visibility.

At the end of Sargent Drive, turn right onto Route 198. There is no shoulder on this road either, but the straightaway gives good visibility for passing cars. Ride 1.3 miles to the Parkman Mountain parking lot, located at the top of the hill on the left.

Enter the carriage road system and turn left at Post 13, riding the gradual incline of Parkman Mountain. After you take a right at Post 12, you will cross two granite bridges, Deer Brook Bridge and the Waterfall Bridge. The road then begins a sloping downhill grade that lasts for about a mile. Turn right at Post 19, and left at Post 18, which brings you to Brown Mountain Gatehouse on Route 198.

Take a left onto Route 198. You may go back to Northeast Harbor one of two ways: The first and most direct route is to follow Route 198 directly down the hill into town, turning left on Harbor Lane to the municipal parking lot. The second route is strictly for expert, off-road riders and covers some rough but beautiful territory on the top of Schoolhouse Ledge. Ride this route at your own risk. To do so, as you are exiting the carriage road system, take a left onto Route 198. Rather than following the hill all the way down into town, however, turn right at the first and only unmarked gravel road on your right that lies about 200 feet from Brown Mountain Gatehouse. This follows the edge of Lower Hadlock Pond; bear left at the fork in the road and left again at the next fork in the road, passing through a small gravel pit area. Follow the path up and over Schoolhouse Ledge, a bumpy, hang-on ride. The road then slopes down toward Northeast Harbor. The road is only about a mile and concludes at a paved road where you must turn right; this leads to Route 198. Take a left and then a right onto Harbor Lane, finishing at the municipal parking lot.

11

Long Pond Fire Road

5.4 miles (*Easy/Family*)

This ride is an exceptional alternative to the carriage roads, which can be crowded during the peak summer months. A leisurely ride and a picnic along the shore of Long Pond make for a relaxing day in the Maine woods.

Traveling by car from Route 102 in Somesville, bear right at the yellow blinking light; this road is also Route 102, and forms a continuous loop around the western side of the island. When you have come 5.9 miles from the intersection, turn right at the Pretty Marsh Picnic Area and park your car. The entrance to the Long Pond Fire Road is 0.1 mile down the hill on the left.

The Long Pond Fire Road, like other fire roads within Acadia National Park, has a smooth gravel surface and is accessible by motor vehicles. The speed limit, however, is only 15 mph, so any rare traffic that you encounter will be driving slowly.

The hills along the first 1.75 miles of dense pine forest give

MAP 11: LONG POND FIRE ROAD

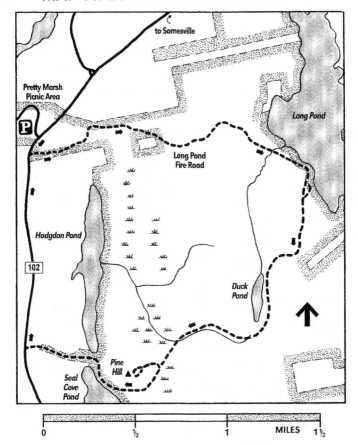

to Somesville

Pretty Marsh
Picnic Area

P

Long Pond

Long Pond
Fire Road

Hodgdon Pond

102

Duck
Pond

Pine
Hill

Seal
Cove
Pond

0   ½   1   MILES   1½

way to the southern shore of Long Pond for a short distance. If you haven't already picnicked at Pretty Marsh, then this would be the place to sit, relax, and dangle your feet in the cool lake water. It is the tranquility of such freshwater habitats on Mount Desert Island that calm calculating minds.

When you are ready to resume your ride, you'll follow more sloping, hilly terrain through the pines. About 1.75 miles from the shore of Long Pond is an intersection where the road joins another, wider fire road. Here you can make a short detour up Pine Hill. If you choose to continue on the main route, take a left instead and follow the road over the bridge that crosses the outlet of Hodgdon Pond. This segment of road is remarkably similar to the carriage roads, complete with "Rockefeller's teeth"—granite coping stones that landscape the edge of the road.

The fire road finally merges with a residential road and then again intersects with Route 102. Turn right onto Route 102, but be cautious; this segment of paved road has no shoulder, and traffic is generally fast. Ride about a mile past charming residences back to the Pretty Marsh Picnic Area.

12

Seal Cove Road and Route 102A Loop

16 miles (*Moderate*)

The steep barren mountaintops for which Samuel de Champlain named this island l'Isle des Monts Déserts in 1604 do not exist on the southwestern corner of the island. Instead, the terrain on this long "Quiet Side" ride offers an easier 16-mile loop than just about anywhere else on Mount Desert Island. A very early morning ride gives you an opportunity to enjoy the peaceful surroundings; during the day, the roads get busy with traffic.

Begin your ride directly from Southwest Harbor by traveling north on Route 102. Turn left onto Seal Cove Road (a posted sign in the grassy median reads EUGENE NORWOOD SR.). Using this approach, you will conquer the most difficult hill at the beginning of your ride. Follow the Seal Cove Road past the campground and into Acadia National Park, where the paved road gives way to the gravel surface of the fire road system.

Two gravel roads on the right lead to other fire roads, including Western Mountain Road. Continue past both

MAP 12: SEAL COVE/ROUTE 102A LOOP

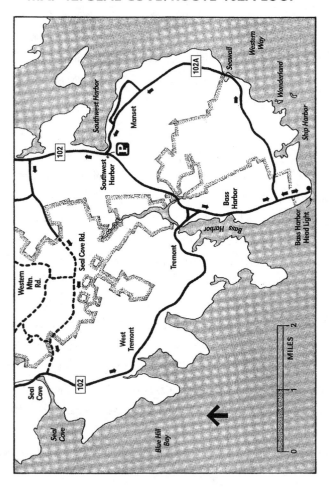

intersections, completing the approximately 3-mile length of Seal Cove Road.

After you leave Acadia National Park, Seal Cove Road ends and intersects with Route 102. Turn left onto Route 102. Rolling hills and curves add character to the paved road through West Tremont and Tremont. Ocean views, saltwater farms, cemeteries, and village churches create a lasting impression of life Down East, past and present.

Just after the second of two bridges at the mouth of Bass Harbor, bear right at the fork in the road. About 0.25 mile down the road, there is a stop sign; turn right. This begins an alternate route, Route 102A, that travels along the southernmost point of Mount Desert Island. At the top of a small rise, you will see signs for Bass Harbor Light. This popular side trip is only about 1 mile.

If you instead choose to stay on Route 102A, follow the left-hand curve in the road. Ship Harbor, Wonderland, and Seawall lie to the right. These areas have short walking trails that lead to the ocean and are worth taking the short detour for a picnic or a break.

After passing Ship Harbor, Wonderland, and Seawall, the road turns slightly inland, meandering through neighborhoods.

At the intersection of Routes 102A and 102, turn right toward Southwest Harbor, at which point you will have completed the loop.

MAP 13: SEAL COVE/WESTERN MOUNTAIN

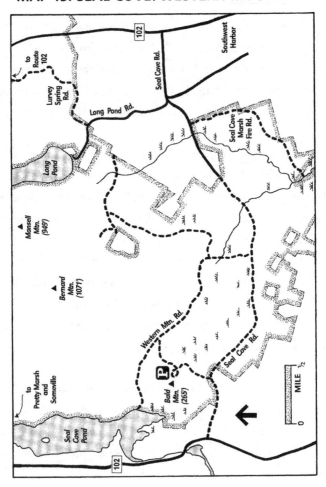

13

Seal Cove and Western Mountain Fire Roads

12 miles, maximum (*Moderate to Difficult*)

The Seal Cove and Western Mountain fire roads, on the west side of Mount Desert Island, are perfect locations to go exploring on your mountain bike. Although there is no loop that completely circumnavigates the area, these directions will guide you into the backwoods and allow you to create divergent routes of your own. Please note that the route can be modified or shortened to better accommodate your riding abilities.

Traveling by car (or by bike if you prefer), turn right at the blinking light in Somesville onto Route 102. About 3.5 miles from the Pretty Marsh Picnic Area, turn left onto Seal Cove Road. After passing through a small residential area, you will enter Acadia National Park. The gravel surface of these fire roads, although still great for mountain biking, is somewhat rougher than the carriage roads because vehicles are allowed.

At the first sign marked WESTERN MOUNTAIN ROAD, turn left and follow the road until you come to Bald Mountain. Turn left again, and park your car at the Bald Mountain parking area.

Ride back down the hill to the first intersection and take a left, following the sign to Southwest Harbor. At the top of a short rise in the road, you will pass a small family cemetery. Another sign farther down the road reads SEAL COVE POND / WESTERN MOUNTAIN ROAD / SOUTHWEST HARBOR.

At this point, the best advice is to have the map on page 62 and a good sense of direction. Each route actually leads to a dead end, but the riding is peaceful and beautiful. Remember that there is no riding on hiking trails. Gear up, and prepare for some fun exploring!

Paved Road Rides

14

Park Loop Road

19 miles (*Moderate to Difficult*)

For bicyclists who enjoy the road-riding experience, Acadia National Park's Loop Road provides a sampling of touring the rocky Maine coastline. This route has the flexibility to be as strenuous or as leisurely a ride as you want to make it. Much of the Park Loop Road is one-way so that vehicles can easily pass, but take note of the posted two-way segments.

This ride is most accessible from Bar Harbor by following Kebo Road to the Park Loop Road. (Take note that the first hill on Kebo Road is a tough one, but it is the most direct, least congested route to the Park Loop Road.) Turn left and follow the one-way road passing the Great Meadow and Sieur de Monts Spring. There is no paved shoulder, so be cautious of passing and parked cars.

MAP 14: PARK LOOP ROAD

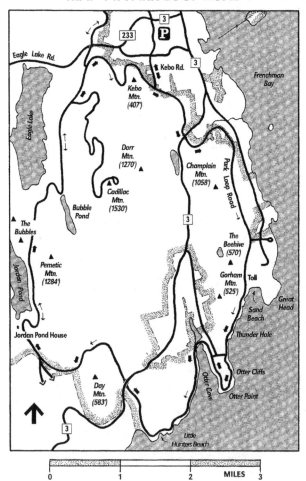

Eagle Lake Rd.

233

3
P

Kebo Rd.

3

Frenchman
Bay

Eagle Lake

Kebo
Mtn.
(407')

Dorr
Mtn.
(1270')

Champlain
Mtn.
(1058')

Park Loop Road

Cadillac
Mtn.
(1530')

Bubble
Pond

The
Bubbles

Pemetic
Mtn.
(1284')

3

The
Beehive
(570')

Jordan Pond

Gorham
Mtn.
(525')

Toll

Great
Head

Sand
Beach

Jordan Pond House

Thunder Hole

Day
Mtn.
(583')

Otter Cliffs

Otter Cove

Otter Point

3

Little
Hunters Beach

0   1   2   MILES   3

The Abbe Museum at Sieur de Monts displays artifacts recovered from the Mount Desert Island region, which was settled by Native American tribes before European colonization. The museum is worth the detour if you are interested in Maine history and archaeology.

The loop continues past Bear Brook Picnic Area. The tough climb up Champlain Mountain gives way to a panoramic view of Egg Rock Light in Frenchman Bay and a long downhill route past the Precipice and Champlain Mountain.

Once you've passed the tollbooth, through which bicyclists are permitted at no charge, you're on what is known as Ocean Drive. The road winds along past rocky shores and headlands, and there are several scenic spots, including Sand Beach, Thunder Hole, and Otter Cliffs. Ride cautiously; traffic tends to be congested along this stretch of road, and drivers—unaware of passing bicyclists—may be pulling into traffic or opening their car doors.

The segment of road that passes Otter Cliffs, Otter Point, Fabbri Memorial, and over the tri-arched granite bridge in Otter Creek shows you a beautiful sample of the Maine coast. The constant motion of the waves keeps the bell buoys ringing out their warnings to fishermen pulling traps. Waves splash the rocks while visitors comb the beaches, enjoying the sights or searching for treasures. Touring the seashore this way, by bicycle, not only gives you great exercise, fun, and a healthy dose of fresh air, but you also get to be part of the landscape! Maybe someone else will get the idea that alternative transportation is something they'd like to try on their next vacation.

About 3 miles from Otter Cliffs is a granite bridge with a small wooden staircase leading down to Hunter's Beach. This is a beautiful rocky beach tucked away from the road—a great spot for a break on a summer day.

After that, much of the ride winds through evergreen forest. Shortly after you pass Wildwood Stables, the one-way road becomes two-way. Jordan Pond House is a wonderful spot to stop and fill your water bottle and maybe even sit down to enjoy afternoon tea and popovers.

As you resume your ride, there are several long climbs, each with the reward of a downhill. Once past Bubble Pond, however, there is a longer climb up the side of Cadillac Mountain. After a short downhill, bear right at the fork in the Park Loop Road; you will pick up the one-way road passing the Gorge Path. Take the first unmarked road on the left, Kebo Road, and continue all the way into town.

If, instead, you bear left at the fork, take your first right at the triangle, another right, and a left onto Eagle Lake Road, following the signs that lead back into Bar Harbor.

Note that there is no swimming allowed at Eagle Lake, Bubble Pond, or Jordan Pond.

15

Whitney Farm and Indian Point Road

11.9 mile loop on paved roads (*Moderate*)

The village of Somesville was the first established township on Mount Desert Island. Located at the head of Somes Sound, the village is representative of life in the past century. The school-house, carriage houses, churches, the old general store, and library still exist, although some have been changed into other businesses or residences. The quaint duck pond and picturesque arched white wood bridge are complementary sights at the starting point of a ride that is both beautiful and challenging.

Take Route 102 into Somesville. Park at the small parking area located at the corner of Route 102 and Oak Hill Road, across from the library and Duck Pond outlet.

The ride begins on Oak Hill Road. Warm up a bit before you depart, as there is a brief climb at the very start. Overall, though, the loop offers sloping downhill runs and short, quick climbs. Ride on Oak Hill Road for 1.4 miles, passing Somes Pond on the left, marshlands on the right, and several residences, some of which are original farmhouses, set amid fields and woods.

MAP 15: WHITNEY FARM/INDIAN POINT ROAD

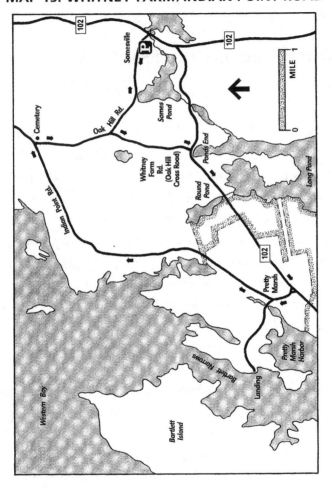

At Whitney Farm Road, take a left. Newer homes have been built in the fields that were once farmland along this 1.1-mile road.

The road ends at the intersection of Route 102. At this point, you will see Pond's End, the boat landing for Long Pond. Take a right, and ride on Route 102. The sloping road takes you through peaceful countryside, past Round Pond on the right, marshlands, and woodlands.

Take a right at the sign marked PRETTY MARSH, and at the next stop sign bear right again onto Indian Point Road. (Before turning onto Indian Point Road, you can take a short detour by continuing straight ahead to Bartlett's Landing. The boat landing is about 2 miles down and back.)

On the 4.7-mile segment of Indian Point Road, the open fields of Gray Farm on the left give way to dense pine forest on both sides of the road where several residences lie tucked into the landscape. This stretch of Indian Point Road is hilly, and there are a couple of demanding climbs.

At Oak Hill Road (marked by the Higgins Family Cemetery), take a right and ride the entire length of Oak Hill Road back to the parking lot in Somesville.

The paved surfaces of this ride are in generally good condition. These roads do not have shoulders or bike lanes, so be sure to ride with the traffic and use hand signals when turning.

MAP 16: WEST SIDE RIDE

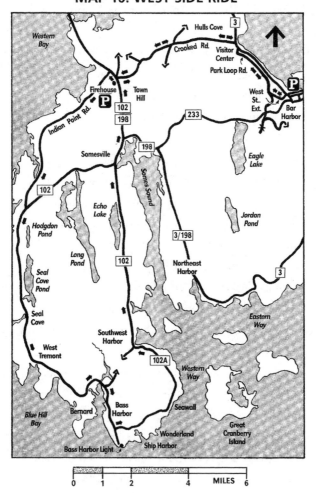

16

The West Side Ride

48.7 miles (*Difficult/Expert*)

A local group of serious cyclists mapped this route for their regular weekend workout for the off-season, but any day of the week is good for this long tour. Some of these roads are heavily trafficked, especially during the summer, so an early-morning start would be to your advantage. The ride can be shortened to 32.7 miles by parking at the Town Hill Fire House and riding just the western side of the island.

Starting from Bar Harbor, take West Street Extension to the Park Loop Road. Turn right and ride to the intersection at the Acadia Visitors Center in Hulls Cove. Turn left onto Route 3 and ride down the hill, where you will turn left again onto the Crooked Road. Some lovely old farms dot the landscape along this 4.8-mile residential stretch of road, including the old Stone Barn Farm at the intersection of the Crooked Road and Norway Drive.

At the intersection of the Crooked Road and Routes 102/198 in Town Hill, turn right and follow the curve in the road to the left for 0.3 mile, then turn left onto Indian Point Road. Like most of the other rural roads on the island, this one doesn't have a shoulder, but the paved road is bordered by evergreen forest, offering a peaceful setting for a road ride. Follow the 5.9-mile Indian Point Road for its entirety.

At the stop sign, turn left and ride for 0.2 mile to the fork in the road. Bear right, which will put you onto Route 102. The traffic on this road is faster; again, there is no shoulder, so ride with caution. This begins the segment that meanders through the west side of the island. Village churches, B&Bs, and antiques shops are all part of the quiet charm. You will pass through the villages of Seal Cove, West Tremont, and Tremont.

Just beyond the turn-off for Bernard, two small bridges cross inlets at the mouth of Bass Harbor. Once you have crossed the second bridge, bear right at the fork in the road and right again at the stop sign at Route 102A through Bass Harbor.

Follow the curve in the road to the left in Bass Harbor; going straight ahead leads to Bass Harbor Head Light. Pass by Ship Harbor, Wonderland, and the Seawall campground and picnic area. As you ride the curving road over the natural rock seawall, you'll see glimpses of Western Way and Great Cranberry Island to the right. The remainder of Route 102A travels through residential areas.

At the stop sign, turn right onto Route 102, following the sign that reads ELLSWORTH. Route 102 travels through Southwest Harbor and Somesville. Go straight at the traffic light and ride back to Town Hill. Turn right onto the Crooked Road, and retrace the beginning of the route back to Bar Harbor.

17

Bar Harbor to Sand Beach and Schooner Head

9 miles (*Moderate*)

This shorter excursion is a way to enjoy both the Park Loop Road and the quiet Schooner Head Road. And you can ride directly from Bar Harbor—a scenic route to Sand Beach.

At the intersection of Routes 3, 233, and Kebo Road in Bar Harbor, take Kebo Road out of town, crossing over Cromwell Harbor Road, to the Park Loop Road. (The first hill up Kebo Road is steep, but it is the most direct, least congested route to follow.) Take a left onto the Park Loop Road and follow it for 3.5 miles. Along the way, you will pass Sieur de Monts Spring, Bear Brook Picnic Area, Beaver Dam Pond, Frenchman Bay Overlook, and Champlain Mountain.

Just before the tollbooth onto the Ocean Drive segment of the Park Loop Road, turn left, following the signs for Schooner Head Overlook. Riding 0.15 mile in on this side road will bring you to a three-way junction. By turning right, you'll continue on

MAP 17: SAND BEACH AND SCHOONER HEAD

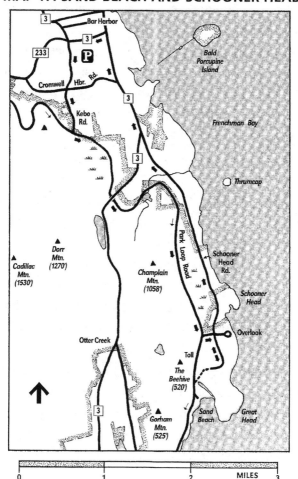

MILES

0   1   2   3

to Sand Beach. Going straight brings you to the Schooner Head Overlook for a beautiful vista. A left turn onto Schooner Head Road will return you to Bar Harbor.

If you choose to go to Sand Beach, turn right and follow the paved road all the way to the end, passing the Great Head parking lot. The paved road narrows to a paved bicycle path and exits onto the Park Loop Road just before the Sand Beach entrance.

On your way back from Sand Beach, return on the bike path that you entered on. At the intersection, cross the street and begin heading back to Bar Harbor via Schooner Head Road. (You will be pedaling through a residential area, so please be respectful of this.)

Schooner Head road offered one of the very first bicycling paths on Mount Desert Island. The outline of the elevated bike path can still be seen on the western side of the road, although it has been more than eighty years since it was used as a bicycle route.

At the end of Schooner Head Road, turn right onto Route 3 headed for Bar Harbor. This stretch of road is a bike route, but avoid riding directly over wastewater drains that could catch your front tire. Follow Route 3 past the ball field and into town, where a left on Mt. Desert Street will lead back to where you started.

18

Schooner Head Road to Otter Cliffs Loop

12 miles (*Moderate*)

This road ride incorporates the most dramatic segment of the Park Loop Road: Ocean Drive and Otter Cliffs. Accessing the route from Schooner Head Road offers more moderate terrain with which to begin your ride.

Starting from the town of Bar Harbor (parking is available at the ball field), travel south on Route 3; there is paved shoulder along this segment. When you have come 0.9 mile from the ball field at the top of the hill, turn left onto Schooner Head Road. This road borders the eastern shoreline of the island, but because of its lower elevation there is actually no view of the ocean. The tree-lined road offers other attractions, however, including lovely views of a beaver pond on your right and of the Precipice from across the meadow.

Ride on Schooner Head Road for the entire 2.5 miles to the stop sign at the end of the road. Turn right and ride for 0.15

MAP 18: SCHOONER HEAD/OTTER CLIFFS LOOP

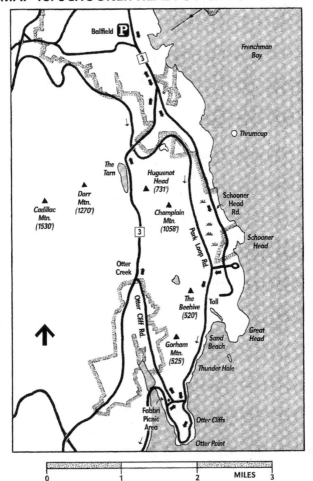

Ballfield 🅿

Frenchman
Bay

3

○ Thrumcap

The
Tarn

Huguenot
Head
(731')

Schooner
Head
Rd.

▲ Dorr
Mtn.
(1270')

▲ Cadillac
Mtn.
(1530')

Champlain
Mtn.
(1058')

3

Schooner
Head

Park Loop Rd.

Otter
Creek

Otter Cliff Rd.

The
Beehive
(520')

Toll

Great
Head

Gorham
Mtn.
(525')

Sand
Beach

Thunder Hole

Fabbri
Picnic
Area

Otter Cliffs

Otter Point

0   1   2   MILES   3

mile to the Park Loop Road. Turn left onto the Park Loop Road and pass through the tollbooth; there is no charge for bicyclists in Acadia National Park. Follow this stretch of road up the hill past Sand Beach and along Ocean Drive. Be cautious of cars parking or pulling into traffic.

As you follow the signs for Otter Cliffs, the road rises to a steeper grade until it splits into two segments. Staying to the right puts you on the upper-level road. All traffic merges again, and you will be riding along the tip of Otter Point. Sweeping views of Otter Cove and the outer bay dominate the landscape.

At the signs for Fabbri Memorial Picnic Area, turn right. Follow the straight stretch for 0.1 mile to the end. Turn left onto Otter Cliff Road, which is lined by woods and residences. Follow the road for its entirety. A steep incline is followed by a sharp curve in the road to the left.

At the stop sign, turn right onto Route 3. The next mile is all downhill. Dorr Mountain and The Tarn appear on your left as you follow the curve in the road around the base of Huguenot Head. You will pass another entrance to Acadia National Park, and Jackson Laboratory further down the road. Route 3 continues past your original turn-off at the Schooner Head Road and leads back down the hill into Bar Harbor.